8.50
brt
4-6-87

D1568841

★★★ *Baseball's* ★★★
WORST TEAMS

★★★ Baseball's ★★★
WORST TEAMS

Nate Aaseng

Lerner Publications Company
Minneapolis

ACKNOWLEDGEMENTS: The photographs are reproduced through the courtesy of: pp. 1, 6, 10, 13, 14, 15, 18, 20 (bottom left & right), 21, 22, 23, 24, 26, 28, 29, 30, 31, 34, 36, 37, 38, 39, 40, 44, 45, 46, 47, 48, 50, 52, 53, 54, 55, 56, 58, 60, 63, 64, 66, 68, 71, National Baseball Hall of Fame and Museum, Inc.; pp. 2, 8-9, 16, 32, 42, AP/Wide World Photos; p. 61, Rochester *Times-Union*. Front cover: Rochester *Times-Union* (left); National Baseball Hall of Fame and Museum, Inc. (right, top & bottom). Back cover: National Baseball Hall of Fame and Museum, Inc.

Back cover: Although they may have wished that the evidence had been destroyed, the men in this picture can't deny they were part of the fiasco known as the original New York Mets.

Page 1: During his playing days, Casey Stengel was known as baseball's foremost clown. It was fitting that he was chosen to direct the comedy of errors that played at the Polo Grounds in New York in 1962.

Page 2: Philadelphia's Clay Dalrymple slaps the tag on a Cardinal runner at the plate in a May 1961 game. Unfortunately, the ball has popped out of his mitt. The Phils walked away empty handed from most of their games that summer.

To my present softball team, which appears to have used the teams in this book as role models

Library of Congress Cataloging-in-Publication Data

Aaseng, Nathan.
    Baseball's worst teams.

    (Sports talk)
    Summary: The author profiles what he considers to be
the eight worst teams in the history of major league
baseball.
    1. Baseball—United States—Clubs—History—Juvenile
literature. [1. Baseball—History] I. Title.
II. Series.
GV875.A1A23   1986   796.357′64′0973   84-23337
ISBN 0-8225-1527-X (lib. bdg.)

Manufactured in the United States of America

1 2 3 4 5 6 7 8 9 10 96 95 94 93 92 91 90 89 88 87 86

★★★ Contents ★★★

Cy Young ranks as the winningest pitcher in baseball history. Few realize that he also pitched for the Cleveland Spiders just one year before their total collapse in 1899.

Introduction

There isn't the same risk involved in choosing baseball's worst teams as there is in ranking its best. After all, who's going to complain if they get left out? Such ragtag outfits as the 1952 Pittsburgh Pirates and the 1936 Boston Braves would be relieved that they had not been lumped with the rest of the teams in this book.

Ordinarily, we're not that interested in losing teams. But if you're looking for truly unbelievable performances, you'll find just as many on the bottom end of the scale as on the top. In fact, the record shows that there have been more wretched teams than great ones. The modern major league record for wins in a season is 116, with the next best total being 111. In this book, you'll find a team with 117 losses, one with 120, and another with 132! Some of the pitching, batting, and fielding records have been so bad that they seem like typographical errors.

What makes one team a proud champion while another team has to slink back to their dugout after most games under the insults of fans? The usual answer is simply that pro sports teams need money to compete. Those who haven't had it have often had to pay a long and embarrassing price. But other factors such as bad luck, revenge, league decisions, rebuilding, and just plain poor judgement have added to the disaster, too.

Some of the statistics in this book make the players seem ridiculous. But the players are the victims, not the villains, of most of these stories. None of the eight teams made this book through lack of effort, and none of the players chose their teammates. Most were fairly skilled players cast in hopeless circumstances. Capable backup players were forced to start, starters were forced to change positions, youngsters were rushed into the majors before they were ready, and aged veterans tried to squeeze one last year into their careers. Their mistake was in signing with owners who either did not want, could not afford,

7

or simply did not know how to build a winner.

When people get swamped by bad luck, the result can be either tragic or comic. The New York Mets showed that, with a little sympathy and a sense of humor, even a pathetic team can draw millions of fans. What made the Mets so fascinating was that they seemed so human. We've all been caught in situations where the whole world seemed bent on making us look silly. Because of that, most of us have had a soft spot for a team like the Mets. Take a sympathetic look, now, at ball players who were trapped on the worst teams the game has ever seen. In the spirit of the teams in this book, the chapters go from bad to worse.

In 1962 this scene showing the Mets' 1969 World Series victory celebration would have been impossible to imagine.

In 1955 fans flocked to Kansas City's Municipal Stadium (above) to welcome their first major league baseball team. Or so they thought. Many would argue that their new team was little more than a Yankee farm club.

★★★1★★★

The Team
That Couldn't Beat the Leftovers

The 1961 Kansas City A's

The fighting Oakland A's of the 1970s would have choked on their breakfast if they had come across a 1961 *Sports Illustrated* article. The article described Charles Finley as "the kindliest owner in the game." It seemed as though there was nothing the A's new owner wouldn't do for his players. Yet within 10 years, Finley owned the angriest group of men in the game. When free agency came to baseball in the mid-1970s, the A's dashed away from Finley like rats scrambling out of a flooded basement. No one knows for sure what caused this huge change, but it could have been that the strain of the 1961 season had its effect. After all, a person can only take so much frustration!

Compared to other teams in this book, the A's 1961 record actually seems respectable. Kansas City won a good deal more often than did some teams who are not in this book, like the 1952 Pirates or the 1935 Braves, but the A's were playing in the golden age of awful teams: losing just wasn't as easy as it was in other years!

The A's, however, did suffer through an unlikely embarrassment. When the American League added two teams in 1961, Kansas City had a great chance for its best record in years. These expansion clubs were so poorly stocked with leftovers from other clubs that one of them was called an "elephant grave-yard." But Kansas City was not able to beat out either of them, and only some good luck enabled them to tie the Washington Senators for ninth place at the end of the year.

The season cannot be blamed on owner Finley, who happened to buy the club before the season started. The team had a losing tradition that had

During his stormy years as owner of the A's, Charles Finley introduced mechanical rabbits, colorful uniforms, and the designated hitter.

started many years before. During the 1930s and 1940s, Connie Mack had guided the Philadelphia A's to 13 straight losing seasons. Arnold Johnson, who had bought the club and moved it to Kansas City in 1955, could do no better. In fact, the A's began to look like a New York Yankee farm club. Mysteriously, Kansas City's best players wound up in Yankee pinstripes. Over a four-year period, the two teams made 16 trades involving 59 players. The result was that New York kept on winning, and the A's kept on losing.

Finley bought a team that had finished in its usual last-place spot in 1960. The Kansas City fans, who had shown much patience up until then, were starting to get bored. Finley meant to change that, and fans began to perk up when he announced a "bus burning." The A's torched an old bus to show that the "shuttle bus" between New York and Kansas City was no longer in operation.

The new owner brought in all sorts of plans to bring baseball up to date in Kansas City. He spruced up the ballpark with improvements and included some picnic grounds beyond the left-field fence. He installed "Little Blowhard," a network of air ducts that could blow the dirt off of home plate. Umpires in Kansas City no longer needed a pouch full of new baseballs. Whenever an old ball went out of play, Harvey, a mechanical rabbit, popped out of the ground to supply a new one.

The A's needed all the gimmicks they could find because the team didn't seem likely to provide much entertainment. There were some hopeful signs of improvement, however, especially in the infield. Ex-Yankees Norm Siebern and Jerry Lumpe both could hit for high

Jerry Lumpe (above) made the mistake of slipping to a .222 average for the powerful New York Yankees and was quickly shipped to Kansas City. Shortstop Dick Howser (right) erased many of the bad memories of 1961 by managing the Kansas City Royals to a World Series title in 1985.

average, and rookie Dick Howser had ability at shortstop. In some of their early games in 1961, the A's looked like world beaters. For example, they had walked all over Minnesota in a 20-2 romp in April. Convinced that tender treatment would bring great efforts from his men, Finley played the generous boss. He took them to dinner and gave struggling players every chance to make the team.

In reality, however, the capable infield unit and all of the ballpark gadgets were just window dressing to cover up a poor team. Most teams looked to their outfield for power hitting; the A's were happy if they could find three bunters who could fill those positions. Leo Posada, Bobby Del Greco, and rookie Deron Johnson were hardly candidates for the All-Star game. The catching was even shakier. The best of the group was Haywood Sullivan, who had batted all of .161 with the Red Sox in 1960.

On top of that, the A's pitching seemed to get worse all the time. Kansas City hurlers had shut out opponents only four times in 1960, and they would be hard pressed to equal that in 1961. Veterans Bud Daley, Ray Herbert, Dick Hall, and Don Larsen were all traded off by midseason. Replacing them were rookies Norm Bass and Jim Archer; Joe Nuxhall, who had been 1-8 with the Cincinnati Reds in 1960; and Bob Shaw, who had been enjoying a decent career with the White Sox before being traded to the A's. In all, the A's tried 22 pitchers from 18-year-old Lew Krausse to 40-year-old Gerry Staley without much luck.

Jim Archer never won another pro game after his rookie season with Kansas City.

By midseason the glow over the Kansas City stadium was replaced by gloom. The club was struggling to stay out of last place when manager Joe Gordon was fired. The impatient Finley then dumped general manager Frank Lane, but the changes didn't help. Quickly they rolled into the cellar far behind either of the new teams, the Angels and the Senators.

Kansas City spent nine straight weeks in last place trying to find a way out. But they had so little leadership that Dick Howser, a *rookie*, had been selected team captain. As the summer drew to a close, it seemed it would take a miracle for Kansas City to avoid being the first 10th-place team in modern baseball. They were saved, however, by a total collapse of the Senators. When Washington lost top pitcher Dick Donovan to injury, they lost 24 out of 25 games to join Kansas City in the cellar. A loss by the Senators on the final day of the year put the teams tied at 61-100, 47½ games behind the Yankees.

Did the A's finally outfox the Yankees when they aquired capable first baseman Norm Siebern? Hardly. In order to get Siebern, the A's had to give up Roger Maris, who blasted 61 home runs for New York in 1961.

In the American League, it had been the year of the home run everywhere except in Kansas City. While Roger Maris cracked out 61 homers for the Yankees, and Mickey Mantle, 54, the A's as a team hit only 90. Norm Siebern led the club with 18; no one else had more than 8. Kansas City's outfield produced averages such as .185, .208, .216, and .230, and home run totals of 8, 7, 5, and 4. Fielding was also well below average, with shortstop Howser kicking in with a league-leading 38 errors.

But it was the pitching staff that was mostly responsible for the poor showing. Only Bass and Archer completed more than four games. Kansas City's combined ERA of 4.74 was by far the highest in the league, a full .72 above the league average.

This combination of weak hitting and poor pitching erased a remarkable showing by the Kansas City infielders. Led by Siebern's .296 and Lumpe's .293, the foursome batted for a higher average than any other infield group in the league. But Kansas City had too many problems to overcome. The efforts of the infielders were lost in the bottom line that said the Kansas City A's could not beat out either expansion team.

Even steady second baseman Jerry Lumpe occasionally stooped to the level of his teammates. Here he sheepishly chases down the ground ball that got through his legs.

THE 1961 KANSAS CITY A'S

Losing Season Streak: 1955-1967   13 years
Last Place Streak: 1960-1961   2 years

1961 Record: 61-100 (47.5 games behind New York Yankees)

	R*	OR	BA	HR	SB	E	CG	ShO	ERA
New York	827	612	.263	240	28	124	47	14	3.46
Detroit	841	671	.266	180	98	146	62	12	3.55
Baltimore	691	588	.254	149	39	128	54	21	3.22
Chicago	765	726	.265	138	100	128	39	**3**	4.06
Cleveland	737	752	.266	150	**34**	139	35	12	4.15
Boston	729	792	.254	112	56	144	35	6	4.29
Minnesota	707	778	.250	167	47	174	49	14	4.28
Los Angeles	744	784	.245	189	37	**192**	**25**	5	4.31
Washington	**618**	776	**244**	119	81	156	39	8	4.23
Kansas City	683	**863**	.247	**90**	58	175	32	5	**4.74**

Starting Lineup:		Position	Bat Average	HR	Errors
	Norm Siebern	lB	.296	18	11
	Jerry Lumpe	2B	.293	3	18
	Dick Howser	SS	.280	3	38**
	Wayne Causey	3B	.276	8	14
	Deron Johnson	RF	.216	8	6
	Bobby Del Greco	CF	.230	5	3
	Leo Posada	LF	.253	7	6
	Haywood Sullivan	C	.242	6	7

**most in league at that position

Starting Pitchers:		Wins	Loses	ERA	Saves
	Norm Bass	11	11	4.69	
	Jim Archer	9	15	3.20	
	Bob Shaw	9	10	4.31	
	Jerry Walker	8	14	4.82	
	Bud Daley	4	8	4.95	
Relief Pitchers:	Joe Nuxhall	5	8	5.34	1
	Bill Kunkel	3	4	5.18	4
	Ed Rakow	2	8	4.76	1

* R=Runs Scored, OR=Opponents' Runs Scored, BA=Batting Average, HR=Home Runs, SB=Stolen Bases, E=Errors,
CG=Complete Games, ShO=Shutouts, ERA=Earned Run Average. **League's worst totals are shown in boldface type.**

After decades of trading away great players, Boston dealt for Detroit's powerful Dale Alexander. Unfortunately, Alexander's lifetime .331 batting average couldn't make up for his defensive problems.

★★★ 2 ★★★
The House That Ruth Left

The 1932 Boston Red Sox

It's ironic that one of the men most often credited with building baseball's greatest team knew or cared little about the game. Harry Frazee's role in stocking the 1927 Yankees and in building a long line of Yankee champs is especially odd because he was the owner of the Boston Red Sox at the time! During Frazee's seven years with the Red Sox, his wheeling and dealing to stay ahead of the bill collectors turned the Yankees into the richest and most successful team in the game and guaranteed the Red Sox a long stay in last place.

From 1922 to 1932, the Red Sox finished last 9 of 11 seasons. During the eight years from 1925 to 1932, the team *averaged* over 100 losses per year! It was not until a free-spending millionaire took over the team in 1933 that Boston finally climbed out of the pit that Frazee had dug.

The problem with Harry Frazee was that he loved the theater far more than he did baseball. In order to pay debts that his theater productions ran up, he sold off ball players. And, since the Red Sox were the World Series champs when he bought the club in 1916, there were plenty of top players to sell. In a case of killing the goose that laid the golden egg, Frazee shipped off pitchers Carl Mays, Herb Pennock, Waite Hoyt, and Bullet Joe Bush, shortstop Everett Scott, third baseman Joe Dugan, and more. But the worst mistake of all was selling pitcher-slugger Babe Ruth. Ruth became the biggest crowd attracter the game had ever known and made a fortune for the Yankees.

Red Sox fans, meanwhile, grew more bitter with each trade. There was celebrating in the city when Frazee finally sold the club in 1923, but the damage

Most baseball owners would consider it a dream come true to have three Hall of Fame pitchers on their staff. But not Harry Frazee (page 20, top left), who sold Waite Hoyt (page 20, bottom), Babe Ruth (page 20, right), and Herb Pennock (above) to keep the bill collectors away.

had already been done. The Red Sox had few capable players left. Matters turned worse when Winslow Palmer, the millionaire who was to supply the money for the Red Sox recovery, died only two years after taking over from Frazee. Left with no players and no money, the Red Sox scrambled to stay afloat.

By that time, the Red Sox should have been suspicious about any deals with the Yankees, but they agreed to another trade in 1930. It seemed like a minor deal at the time. Boston swapped Red Ruffing, who had lost 47 games for them in two years, to New York for an aging reserve player. But Ruffing came alive to post four 20-win seasons for the Yankees on his way to the Hall of Fame, which caused Red Sox fans to howl again.

Whatever the Red Sox tried, they only settled more deeply into last place. For the 1932 season, the goal was to get more offense. Boston traded for a pair of hard-hitting giants, Dale Alexander and Smead (Smudge) Jolley. Alexander was a 6-foot, 3-inch, 210-pounder who hit well for the Detroit Tigers. Unfortunately, he did not field well enough to assure himself a spot in the Tiger line-

Earlier season reinforcements arrived in the form of hard-hitting outfielders Smead Jolley (above) and Roy Johnson (page 23, left). But that still left the Red Sox outmanned at all positions.

up. Jolley, obtained from the White Sox, was nearly a carbon copy of Alexander in size and ability. Boston also dealt for veteran catcher Bennie Tate from the White Sox and outfielder Roy Johnson from the Tigers, which gave them four reliable batters.

There was nothing else in the Boston lineup for opposing pitchers to fear. The best of the leftovers was center fielder Rebel Oliver, who had hit .276 in 1931 with no home runs. Rounding out the infield were Rabbit Warstler, a third-year shortstop; second-year man Urbane Pickering at third base; and second-year second baseman Marv Olson. For lack of a better place to put him, Alexander was put on first base.

Boston's pitching staff had been a two-man show. Danny MacFayden had somehow gone 16-12 in 1931, and Wilcy Moore, 11-13. Moore had learned first-hand about the steep ups and downs of baseball, as he had been the star reliever on the great 1927 Yankee team before winding up with the Red Sox. The rest of the pitching staff ranged from poor to awful.

Despite their improved offense, the Red Sox got off to a bad start. After

Marty McManus brought the Red Sox out of a tailspin that was leading them to the American League's all-time worst record. After he took over as manager, the team "rallied" to a 32-65 finish.

winning only 11 of their first 57 games, manager Shano Collins was fired. The pitching collapsed when the two "dependable" men, MacFayden and Moore, had trouble getting anyone out and were traded in midseason. Despite little hope for improvement, Marty McManus managed the team well enough to avoid the league record for losses.

With a team batting average of .251, the Red Sox seemed to have at least boosted their offense. But a closer look shows that this was a full 26 points

The only luck to be found on the team settled on Bob Kline. Despite a hefty 5.28 earned run average, he won 11 games for the Red Sox. Two years later, Kline was wallowing in good fortune when he allowed more than seven runs a game yet led the league with seven relief wins!

below the league average! Considering that Dale Alexander led the league with .372 and was backed up by Jolley's .309 and Roy Johnson's .299, it was obvious that the rest of the lineup was not much help. Despite Alexander's and Jolley's impressive hitting, experts claimed that the Red Sox had erred in trading for them. Both were such clumsy fielders that, within a couple of years, they had fumbled their way out of the majors.

Boston's pitching staff, which had been stripped of three Hall of Fame throwers in the last 11 years, posted a hefty 5.02 ERA. Despite his 5.28 ERA, Junior Kline was able to squeeze out 11 wins against 13 losses. Other pitchers such as Ed Durham (6-13, 3.80) and Lefty Weiland (6-16, 4.51) were not so fortunate.

After all of their efforts to improve, the Red Sox ended up with their worst mark of all time: 43-111. That put them a whopping 64 games behind the league-champion Yankees. Fortunately, Tom Yawkey arrived on the scene in 1933 and pumped money into the organization. Instant relief came in the form of the great Lefty Grove, purchased from the Philadelphia A's for the 1934 season. Never again did the Red Sox fall into last place in the league.

The damage caused by the great sell-out of the 1920s has never totally healed, however. For decades, the Red Sox have still been chasing the New York Yankees. While the Yankees have won 22 World Series titles since then, the Red Sox have won none. If only Babe Ruth had stayed with the Red Sox during his whole career!

THE 1932 BOSTON RED SOX

Losing Season Streak: 1919-1933   *15 years*
Last Place Streak: 1925-1930, 1932   *7 of 8 years*

1932 Record: 43-111   (64 games behind New York Yankees)

	R*	OR	BA	HR	SB	E	CG	ShO	ERA
New York	1002	724	.286	160	77	188	95	11	3.98
Philadelphia	981	752	.290	173	**38**	124	95	10	4.45
Washington	840	716	.284	61	70	125	66	10	4.16
Cleveland	845	747	.285	78	52	191	94	6	4.12
Detroit	799	787	.273	80	103	187	67	9	4.30
St. Louis	736	898	.276	67	69	188	63	8	5.01
Chicago	667	897	.267	**36**	89	**264**	50	2	4.82
Boston	**566**	**915**	**.251**	53	46	233	**42**	2	**5.02**

		Position	Bat Average	HR	Errors
Starting Lineup:	Dale Alexander	1B	.372	8	9
	Marv Olson	2B	.248	0	28
	Rabbit Warstler	SS	.211	0	41
	Urbane Pickering	3B	.260	2	21
	Roy Johnson	RF	.299	11	13
	Tom Oliver	CF	.264	0	6
	Smead Jolley	LF	.309	18	15
	Bennie Tate	C	.245	2	8

**most in league at that position

		Wins	Loses	ERA	Saves
Starting Pitchers:	Bob Weiland	6	16	4.51	
	Ed Durham	6	13	3.80	
	Ivy Andrews	8	6	3.81	
	Danny MacFayden	1	10	5.10	
Relief Pitchers:	Bob Kline	11	13	5.28	2
	Wilcy Moore	4	10	5.23	4
	Johnny Welch	4	6	5.23	0

* R=Runs Scored, OR=Opponents' Runs Scored, BA=Batting Average, HR=Home Runs, SB=Stolen Bases, E=Errors, CG=Complete Games, ShO=Shutouts, ERA=Earned Run Average. **League's worst totals are shown in boldface type.**

The stairs to the dressing room seem a mile high as the shell-shocked Phils trudge back to the locker room after absorbing their 19th defeat in a row in 1961. And the nightmare wasn't over yet.

★★★3★★★
Will They Ever Win Again?

The 1961 Philadelphia Phillies

On July 28, 1961, John Buzhardt pitched the Philadelphia Phillies to a 4-3 win over the San Francisco Giants. On August 20, Buzhardt again came through with a 7-4 win over the Milwaukee Braves. Between those games, the Phillies played the worst stretch of baseball since the beginning of the modern era in 1901. Although they did not keep up this self-destruction for the whole year, their streak of 23 straight losses puts them in the company of the game's worst teams.

Like most of the clubs in this book, the Phillies had been turning out poor teams throughout most of their history. No other National League team could match their record of 13 seasons with more than 100 losses. The Phils had surged to win the 1950 pennant with their "Whiz Kids," but they had gone into a long slide afterwards. At the start of the 1960s, Philadelphia again turned to young players to rebuild their fortunes.

The 1960 team was one of the youngest ever to play in the majors, and no one was surprised or upset when they finished last at 59-95. Everyone knew it would take time for their promising players to gain needed experience. Manager Gene Mauch, though, expected the youngsters to make fewer mistakes and win more games in 1961.

There was hope early in the year for this team that had no starting fielders with more than four years experience. Pitcher Art Mahaffey looked like another Sandy Koufax as he struck out 17 Cubs on April 29. By the end of May, Mahaffey was sailing along with a 6-3 mark. Help also arrived early in the year to patch up two weak spots when Philadelphia traded with the Dodgers for third baseman Charlie Smith and outfielder Don Demeter.

"You never learn anything from losing," is a popular saying among managers, but Art Mahaffey might argue with that. Following graduation from the Phillies' 1961 school of hard knocks, Mahaffey won 19 games for Philadelphia in 1962.

That gave the team a sound outfield of Demeter, speedy center fielder Tony Gonzales, and fourth-year outfielder John Callison. All three had hit nine home runs in 1960, but they were capable of at least twice that many.

After his .281 average and 17 homers in 1960, first baseman Pancho Herrera was expected to lead the attack. Tony Taylor at second base was another dependable .280 hitter. Although neither shortstop Ruben Amaro nor catcher Clay Dalrymple were expected to hit for an average higher than their weight, they were able glove men.

Philadelphia also looked forward to a better year from their hurlers. They hoped that Robin Roberts could return to the form that had topped the National League in wins four years in a row (1952-55) and in strikeouts for two straight years (1953-54). The word, however, was that the 14-year veteran was losing his fastball. The Phils also counted on Frank Sullivan to use his menacing 6-foot, 7-inch frame to erase the memory of his 6-16 year in 1960. And just in case these veterans failed, the team had young pitchers like John Buzhardt, Chris Short, and Jack Baldschun in reserve.

Although you couldn't tell it from watching them play, the 1961 Phils were loaded with talent. John Callison (top left) belted 226 homers in his career, plus a game-winning shot in the 1964 All-Stars game. In 1960 Pancho Herrera (top right) hit .281 with 17 home runs. Pitcher Frank Sullivan (bottom left) led the American League in wins in 1955, and Clay Dalrymple (bottom right) hit .276 with 11 home runs in 1962.

One of the "Whiz Kids" who had led the Phillies to the 1950 National League pennant, Robin Roberts suffered through the growing pains of Philadelphia's latest youth movement.

Mahaffey fell into a slump. Things got so bad that the Phils even lost an exhibition game to their class-A farm team. Late in July, the team stumbled through a bad week, losing five of six. As it turned out, though, it was the most successful week they would have in nearly a month!

During the losing streak, the batters came through only once: with eight runs against the Cardinals. Philadelphia walked in the deciding run, however, in a 9-8 loss. After that, Phillie bats returned to the dugout practically unmarked. The team went 9 games in a row with two runs or less and 3 in a row without scoring at all. Among their losses were 4 straight to the Reds, making it 16 straight defeats at the hands of the Cincinnati club.

When the losing streak hit 13 games, Philadelphia got a break from the schedule. Their next 6 games would be against the sixth- and seventh-place teams. Surely, they could win one of them. But the Pirates and Cubs were as eager to play the slumping Phils as the Phils were to play them. After Pittsburgh shut them out twice, the Phils fell victim to the big inning. In the next 4 games,

But as the days grew warmer, the Phils' hopes were buried deeper and deeper. Roberts and Sullivan were getting worse, not better, and even

Fortunately for manager Gene Mauch, nobody blamed him for the team's poor showing. He survived to manage for more than 20 years in the majors.

Phillie foes notched single-inning scores of 8, 5, 4, and 4 runs to blow them off the field. Nothing was going in Gene Mauch's favor, as the manager found out in a brawl against the Pirates. Although the entire roster of players rushed out to join the fight, only one Phillie was hurt: manager Mauch!

The young Phillies tried to keep their spirits up, but the strain began to show. Eight one-run losses and an unending series of bad breaks were too much for Ruben Amaro and Charlie Smith. They put out such effort that they were forced to the bench from exhaustion.

On August 17, Philadelphia set a modern National League record of 20 losses in a row. They had led the Braves, 6-5, in the eighth but could not hold on. The Braves beat them again the next day to give Philadelphia the modern major league mark. Finally on August 20, the Phillies broke through to win the second game of a doubleheader against Milwaukee, 7-4. The runaway losing streak had finally been stopped at 23 games.

The plane returning the team from Milwaukee to Philadelphia was landing when pitcher Sullivan spotted a small crowd waiting for them at the airport. He advised his teammates to leave the plane at one-minute intervals "so they can't get us all in one burst." To the Phils' surprise, they were carried off on the shoulders of the fans, who were just pleased that their team had finally won a game!

With that terrible load finally lifted, the team played well enough in the final month to boost their final record to 47-107. But the effects of the streak

Desperate for victory, Philadelphia tried too hard. Here hustling outfielder John Callison overruns a line drive, which dooms the Phils to consecutive loss number 23.

left them with the league's worst batting average, worst ERA, and a tie for the fewest home runs. Mahaffey lost 10 games in a row to end up with an 11-19 mark. Robin Roberts nearly wrecked his chances of getting into the Hall of Fame with his 1-10 disaster, while Frank Sullivan fell to 3-16.

Tony Gonzales, for lack of competition, took the team batting title with a .277 mark. Of the other starters, only John Callison edged over the .260 level. But the one who most wished he could forget the year was catcher Clay Dalrymple. After ranking dead last in the league in hitting for most of the year, the young receiver led the league's catchers with 14 errors.

Despite the embarrassing season, there was no ranting by the team's owner, and the manager was not fired. The whole mess was calmly chalked up to growing pains of a young team. The Phils, in fact, did prove to have some ability. Of the eight regulars, seven ended up playing at least 10 years in the majors. They probably wouldn't have been upset, however, if 1 of those years, 1961, could have been blotted out of the record book!

THE 1961 PHILADELPHIA PHILLIES

Losing Season Streak: 1958-1961   4 years
Last Place Streak: 1958-1961   4 years

1961 Record: 47-107 (46 games behind Cincinnati Reds)

	R*	OR	BA	HR	SB	E	CG	ShO	ERA
Cincinnati	710	653	.270	158	70	134	46	12	3.78
Los Angeles	735	697	.262	157	86	144	40	10	4.04
San Francisco	773	655	.258	183	79	102	39	9	3.77
Milwaukee	712	656	.258	188	70	111	57	8	3.89
St. Louis	703	668	.271	**103**	46	166	49	10	3.74
Pittsburgh	694	675	.273	128	**26**	150	34	9	3.92
Chicago	689	**800**	.255	176	35	**183**	34	**6**	4.48
Philadelphia	**584**	796	**.243**	103	56	146	**29**	9	**4.61**

		Position	Bat Average	HR	Errors
Starting Lineup:	Pancho Herrera	1B	.258	13	8
	Tony Taylor	2B	.250	2	10
	Ruben Amaro	SS	.257	1	19
	Charley Smith	3B	.248	9	22
	Don Demeter	RF	.257	20	1
	Tony Gonzales	CF	.277	12	4
	John Callison	LF	.266	9	8
	Clay Dalrymple	C	.220	5	14**

**most in league at that position

		Wins	Loses	ERA	Saves
Starting Pitchers:	Art Mahaffey	11	19	4.10	
	John Buzhardt	6	18	4.49	
	Chris Short	6	12	5.94	
	Jim Owens	5	10	4.47	
	Robin Roberts	1	10	5.85	
Relief Pitchers:	Jack Baldschun	5	3	3.88	3
	Frank Sullivan	3	16	4.29	6
	Don Ferrarese	5	12	3.76	1
	Dallas Green	2	4	4.85	1

* R=Runs Scored, OR=Opponents' Runs Scored, BA=Batting Average, HR=Home Runs, SB=Stolen Bases, E=Errors,
CG=Complete Games, ShO=Shutouts, ERA=Earned Run Average. **League's worst totals are shown in boldface type.**

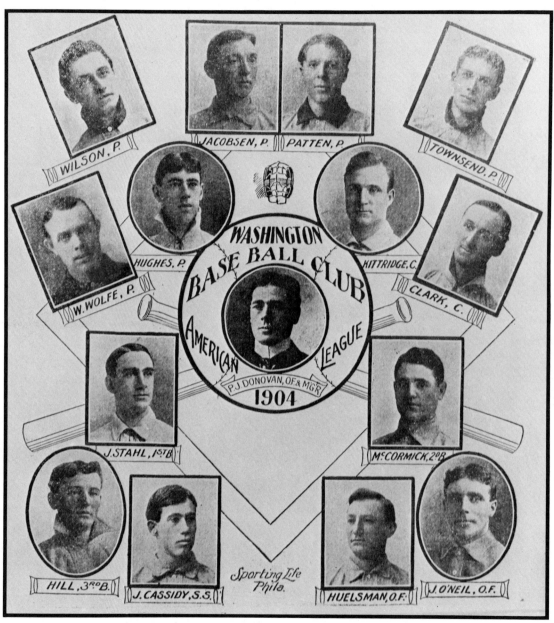

Notice that not one of these 1904 Senators is smiling.
A look at their record may explain why.

4

First in War, First in Peace, and Last in the American League

The 1904 Washington Senators

"First in war, first in peace, and first in the hearts of his countrymen" was a popular phrase to describe George Washington, the first U.S. president. The variation of this phrase that appears in the title of this chapter stuck with the Washington Senators throughout most of their years. Except for a few brief seasons of glory, the residents of the nation's capital suffered along with their home team from the clubs' first game to its last. Among the many bad teams that have worn the Washington uniform, none was worse than the 1904 outfit. That group set a standard for ineptitude that was to become a Senator trademark.

Washington was one of four new clubs brought in to complete the American League in 1901. The new league was determined to compete right away with the National League, and the best way

to do that was to raid the National League teams. In 1901, 111 of the American League's 182 players had jumped over from the National League. The Washington team was not as wealthy as other teams, however, so they were not able to lure away as many stars. As a result, in 1901 and 1902 they finished sixth out of eight teams.

Then a series of strange events took place that sent the Senators deep into last place. One blow was a tragic and mysterious accident that claimed the life of their star, Big Ed Delahanty, the one top National Leaguer the Senators were able to get. In 1902 Delahanty had finished second in the American League with a solid .376 average. Midway through 1903, his .333 average was helping to keep the Senators competitive. But on a July trip, Big Ed caused such a disturbance that he was finally ordered

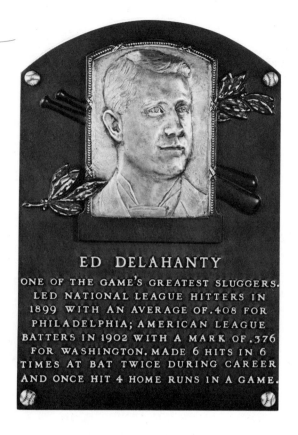

ED DELAHANTY

ONE OF THE GAME'S GREATEST SLUGGERS.
LED NATIONAL LEAGUE HITTERS IN
1899 WITH AN AVERAGE OF .408 FOR
PHILADELPHIA; AMERICAN LEAGUE
BATTERS IN 1902 WITH A MARK OF .376
FOR WASHINGTON. MADE 6 HITS IN 6
TIMES AT BAT TWICE DURING CAREER
AND ONCE HIT 4 HOME RUNS IN A GAME.

off the train he was riding. Ed then apparently pushed his way onto a narrow bridge near Niagara Falls and fell to his death.

An even greater mystery was what happened to three other fine players on the 1901 team. All were young men who seemed to have fine careers in front of them. In 1901 Irv Waldron had batted .322 for the Senators, and Sam Dungan was close on his heels at .320. Shortstop Billy Clingman led the American League in fielding at his important position. But a check of the 1902 rosters shows that all three had disappeared not only from the Senators but from major league baseball.

Washington went to the trading market to find replacements, and they did not set their sights very high. In 1903 they picked up first baseman Jake Stahl and catcher Malachi Kittredge from the Boston Braves. Stahl was coming off a .239 season, and Kittredge had rarely hit better than .220 is his 13-year career. But both won starting jobs for the Senators. Barry McCormick came over from the Browns, and his .216 average was good enough to earn the second-base job.

Right fielder Patsy Donovan, another new arrival from the Browns, seemed like a more sensible addition. An established star, Donovan came to Washington sporting a .327 average. But as he was heading into his final full season in the majors, Washington could hardly be said to have been building for the future. They made another typical trade in 1904 that brought yet another weak hitter to the lineup: third baseman Hunter Hill.

With his .262 average and three home runs, Garland "Jake" Stahl made up the "meat" of Washington's undernourished attack.

Apparently, none of the other teams had any reserve shortstops or center fielders they wanted to get rid of, so Washington was forced to go with rookies Joe Cassidy and Bill O'Neill. The left-field position was given to Frank Huelsman, who was just back into the routine of play after six years away from major league ball.

The pitching staff included only one true major leaguer: Casey Patten. Casey had won 11 and lost 22 in 1903, with an ERA of 3.60. Those figures do not do him justice, though, because his team was shut out in 7 of his losses. Patten could not have looked forward to 1904, as the lineup appeared to be weaker than ever. Joining him on the mound were Jack "Happy" Townshend (who must have earned his nickname before his 1-11 1903 record), Davey Dunkle, and rookie Beany Jacobson.

These men had the privilege of pitching for what was possibly the worst major league batting order ever assembled. The Senators' top hitter in 1904 was Jake Stahl, who paved the way with .262. Rookie Joe Cassidy was the only other infielder to hit better than .218. Even Patsy Donovan suddenly

Manager Patsy Donovan couldn't criticize his players' poor showing. After all, as a starting outfielder, Donovan drove in only 19 runs.

With that kind of support, Casey Patten must have felt like the lone defender at a fort under attack. Casey's team was shut out in 9 of his starts, making a total of 16 games in two years in which his team had failed to score for him. Given the circumstances, his 15-23 record and 3.07 ERA could almost qualify for the Hall of Fame!

Happy Townshend, Beany Jacobson, and Davey Dunkle were not able to perform with such a team. Townshend was 5-26; Jacobson, 6-23; and Dunkle, 1-9. The staff ERA of 3.62 does not seem bad at all, but that was more than one run per game over the league average. The only thing that saved Washington from being worse was the fact that they topped the league in double plays.

The Senators made a clean sweep of all major categories by adding a last place fielding average to their .227 batting mark and battered pitching staff. With so many things against them, they had to scratch and scramble to come up with 38 wins against 113 losses.

It was a long overdue piece of luck that finally pulled the Senators out of their hopeless mess. A traveling salesman stumbled upon a longarmed pitcher

forgot how to swing the bat, and his batting average plunged nearly 100 points to .229. Donovan and Malachi Kittredge each took a turn at managing the club, but there wasn't much they could do. If they were tempted to juggle their lineup, one look at the bench would discourage them. Such colorful names as Boileryard Clark could do no better when they got into a game.

WALTER PERRY JOHNSON
WASHINGTON—1907-1927
CONCEDED TO BE FASTEST BALL PITCHER
IN HISTORY OF GAME. WON 414 GAMES
WITH LOSING TEAM BEHIND HIM MANY YEARS
HOLDER OF STRIKE OUT AND SHUT OUT RECORDS

Pitching for the Senators was like trying to drain a swamp with a bucket! During his first four years with Washington, the great Walter Johnson (left) fired some of the hardest pitches ever thrown yet came away with 32 wins and 48 losses.

in Idaho and alerted the Senators. So it was that Walter Johnson, rated by many the best pitcher the game has ever seen, joined Washington in 1907. For years he was all that stood between the Senators and another disastrous season like 1904. But, as Casey Patten would point out, even the great Johnson would have been hard-pressed to win with the weak-hitting Senators of 1904.

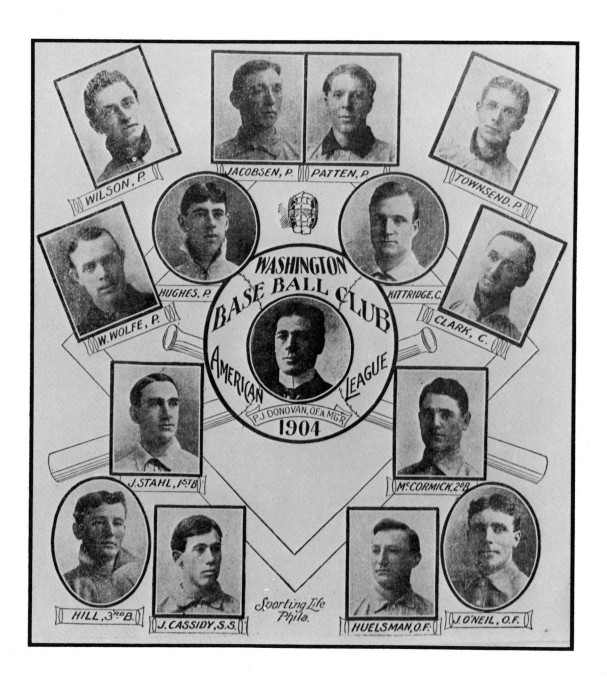

WILSON, P.   JACOBSEN, P.   PATTEN, P.   TOWNSEND, P.

HUGHES, P.   KITTRIDGE, C.

W. WOLFE, P.   CLARK, C.

WASHINGTON BASE BALL CLUB
AMERICAN LEAGUE
P. J. DONOVAN, O.F. & MGR.
1904

J. STAHL, 1ST B.   McCORMICK, 2D B.

HILL, 3RD B.   J. CASSIDY, S.S.   *Sporting Life Philo.*   HUELSMAN, O.F.   J. O'NEIL, O.F.

THE 1904 WASHINGTON SENATORS

Losing Season Streak: 1901-1911   11 years
Last Place Streak: 1903-1904   2 years

1904 Record: 38-113 (55.5 games behind Boston Red Sox)

	R*	OR	BA	HR	SB	E	CG	ShO	ERA
Boston	608	466	.247	26	**101**	242	148	21	2.12
New York	598	526	.259	26	163	275	**123**	15	2.57
Chicago	600	482	.242	14	216	238	134	26	2.30
Cleveland	647	482	.260	27	178	255	141	20	2.22
Philadelphia	557	503	.249	31	137	250	137	26	2.35
St. Louis	481	604	.239	10	150	267	135	13	2.38
Detroit	505	627	.231	11	112	273	143	15	2.77
Washington	**437**	**743**	**.227**	**10**	150	**314**	137	**7**	**3.62**

		Position	Bat Average	HR	Errors
Starting Lineup:	Jake Stahl	1B	.262	3	29**
	Barry McCormick	2B	.218	0	37
	Joe Cassidy	SS	.241	1	37
	Hunter Hill	3B	.197	0	25**
	Patsy Donovan	RF	.229	0	9
	Bill O'Neill	CF	.244	1	18
	Frank Huelsman	LF	.248	2	6
	Malachi Kittredge	C	.242	0	8

**most in league at that position

		Wins	Loses	ERA
Starting Pitchers:	Casey Patten	15	23	3.07
	Jack Townshend	5	26	3.58
	Beany Jacobson	6	23	3.55
	Bill Wolfe	6	9	3.27
	Long Tom Hughes	2	13	3.47
	Davey Dunkle	1	9	4.96

Relief Pitchers: NONE

* R=Runs Scored, OR=Opponents' Runs Scored, BA=Batting Average, HR=Home Runs, SB=Stolen Bases, E=Errors, CG=Complete Games, ShO=Shutouts, ERA=Earned Run Average. **League's worst totals are shown in boldface type.**

It took a world war to get the St. Louis Browns into this World Series in 1944—
the only World Series appearance in their history.

5

Always Poor, Always Unsuccessful, Always Lonely

The 1939 St. Louis Browns

It's often said that the mark of a true champion is the ability to stay on top, year after year. It stands to reason, then, that the test of a *loser* is whether it can remain dismal for years on end. No major league team has ever stood under the cloud of despair longer than the St. Louis Browns. The Browns cranked out one bad season after another so regularly that people rarely noticed them. As far as many fans were concerned, the Browns were only around to fill out the schedule and see that no one else was stuck in last place.

From the club's beginning in 1901 until it finally moved to Baltimore in 1954 to become the Orioles, the Browns won only one pennant. And that was a cheap one in 1944 when most of the better players had joined the armed forces during World War II. Other teams went through hard times, but no matter how bad they were, they usually found the Browns keeping them company at the bottom of the standings. While other fans remembered the glory days of their teams, Browns fans drew a blank. The closest thing they had to a memorable year was a second-place finish in 1922.

The St. Louis Browns were a perfect example of how *not* to run a ball club. It seemed that any trade or business deal they made went sour. When they tried to make money by renting their ballpark to the St. Louis Cardinals, the Cardinals won over the Browns' fans—and the grass was gone by midsummer.

The Browns were caught in a cruel trap. They needed to field a good team in order to draw fans. And they needed to draw fans to get the money to put together a good team. Since the team could never break out of the cycle, they

Bobo Newsom couldn't get any respect. He was traded 16 times in his career—5 times by the same team! (Washington) Despite his 20 wins, even the Browns sent him packing.

were always poor, unsuccessful, and lonely.

One of the Browns' 1933 games was played in the eerie silence of a park that was empty except for 33 paid customers. During all of 1935, they attracted 81,000 fans. (Several modern teams often draw that many in two games.)

In the sad history of the Browns, the lowest point came in 1939. Going into the season, the team was worried about its pitching, and with good reason. Their staff consisted of 20-game winner Bobo Newsom and a collection of batting-practice throwers. Even with Newsom's totals included, their ERA had averaged over 6.00 during the past three years. Unfortunately, in shaking up their pitching staff, the one they let go was Newsom. The Detroit Tigers figured they needed one solid pitcher to put them within reach of the championship. In exchange for Newsom, they agreed to part with four of their hurlers.

At first it seemed the Browns had done a wise thing in sacrificing quality for quantity. Vern Kennedy (12-9 and 5.06 in 1938), George Gill (12-9, 4.12),

Left: Vern Kennedy's promising career fell apart after he joined the Browns. Before the trade, he had won 59 and lost 47 but then dropped to 46-85 afterwards. Manager Fred Haney (above) also had trouble shaking the cloud that hung over the Brown players. After being fired by the Browns, he led Pittsburgh to three last-place finishes before finally winning a pennant with Milwaukee in 1957.

Roxie Lawson, and Bob Harris gave them an instant pitching staff. Together with promising rookie Jack Kramer and the team's strikeout ace, Lefty Mills, the staff looked more settled than it had in years.

Manager Fred Haney could count on good hitting from first baseman George McQuinn and third baseman Harland

Muscles Gallagher didn't hit the long ball the way the Browns were hoping. During his two-year career, he swatted only 16 homers.

Clift. McQuinn had hit .324 with 12 homers in 1938, while Clift had smacked 34 home runs with a .290 average. In addition, the Browns traded for two hard-hitting outfielders: Chet Laabs from Detroit and Joe "Muscles" Gallagher from the Yankees. Rookie Johnny Berardino was counted on to improve play at second base.

All the best-laid plans, however, produced the usual results for the Browns. While Newsom went on to a fabulous career at Detroit, the four ex-Tigers flunked the test at St. Louis. The worst disappointment was George Gill, who nose-dived to a 1-12 record and a generous 7.11 ERA. Vern Kennedy found out what pitching for the Browns could do to a promising career when he fell to 9-17 and 5.73. The other two from Detroit combined for a 6-19 mark. The "bright" spot on the mound was rookie Jack Kramer, who showed ability in his 9-16 season. He would later go on to post an 18-5 record, but, of course, only after he was traded to the Red Sox. Despite their efforts to upgrade the pitching, St. Louis again gave up more than 6 earned runs per game. As usual, that was about 1½ more than the league average.

Jack Kramer bounced back from the 1939 disaster to hurl a shutout in the Browns' suprise World Series appearance in 1944.

Part of the problem may have been a startling lack of balance on the team. Lefty Mills was the only left-handed pitcher, and his 4-11 record and 6.55 ERA wouldn't scare anyone. That meant the Browns had no one to bring in to face a strong left-handed lineup.

The same thing was true of their hitting, as McQuinn was the only lefty. McQuinn must have taken advantage of all of the right-handed pitching the Browns saw, as he hit .316 with 20 homers. But he stood out like a flare from the rest of the Browns. No one else, not even Muscles Gallagher, hit over .300 or had more than 15 home runs. Although the Browns' team average of .268 was far better than the other teams in this book, that number is misleading. The major leagues were in the era of the "live" baseball, when ERAs and averages skyrocketed. Actually, the Browns' hitting was 11 points *below* the league average.

At least the club did not have to suffer its humiliation in public. Their games were quiet affairs. In their last-place effort, the Browns attracted only 109,000 fans. During one game, the visiting Philadelphia A's relief pitchers

47

The 1939 season was a mixed blessing for George McQuinn, who enjoyed his best season during the Browns' worst year.

tried to locate the 150 customers who were announced as the paid attendance. By their count, at least half of the fans must have wandered off in search of food or other entertainment!

That year St. Louis staggered home with an even worse record than usual: 43-111. That put them 64½ games behind the New York Yankees, an American League record that still stands. The Browns' miserable finish moved the league president to act. In 1940 he urged the rest of the league to help out the Browns for the good of baseball. A couple of clubs actually did respond by offering them a player or two at a bargain rate.

But except for the fluke 1944 pennant, the Browns just couldn't escape their fate. The best idea the club ever had came in 1954 when they decided to forget the whole thing and move to Baltimore. Within a decade, the Orioles had grown into one of the best organizations in the game. It could never have happened to the old St. Louis Browns!

THE 1939 ST. LOUIS BROWNS

Losing Record Streak: 1930-1941   12 years
Last Place Streak: 1939   1 year

1939 Record: 43-111 (64.5 games behind New York Yankees)

	R*	OR	BA	HR	SB	E	CG	ShO	ERA
New York	967	556	.287	166	72	126	87	12	3.31
Boston	890	795	.291	124	**42**	180	52	4	4.56
Cleveland	797	700	.280	85	72	180	69	9	4.08
Chicago	755	737	.275	64	113	167	62	5	4.31
Detroit	849	762	.279	124	88	198	64	6	4.29
Washington	**702**	797	.278	**44**	94	205	72	4	4.60
Philadelphia	711	1022	.271	98	60	**210**	**50**	5	5.79
St. Louis	733	**1035**	**.268**	91	48	199	56	**3**	**6.01**

		Position	Bat Average	HR	Errors
Starting Lineup:	George McQuinn	1B	.316	20	11
	Johnny Berardino	2B	.256	5	29**
	Don Heffner	SS	.267	1	21
	Harlord Clift	3B	.270	15	25
	Myril Hoag	RF	.295	10	7
	Chet Laabs	CF	.300	10	6
	Muscles Gallagher	LF	.282	9	9
	Gabber Glenn	C	.273	4	11

**most in league at that position

		Wins	Loses	ERA	Saves
Starting Pitchers:	Jack Kramer	9	16	5.83	
	Vern Kennedy	9	17	5.73	
	Bob Harris	3	12	5.71	
	George Gill	1	12	7.11	
Relief Pitchers:	Lefty Mills	4	11	6.55	2
	Bill Trotter	6	13	5.34	0
	Roxie Lawson	3	7	5.32	0

* R=Runs Scored, OR=Opponents' Runs Scored, BA=Batting Average, HR=Home Runs, SB=Stolen Bases, E=Errors, CG=Complete Games, ShO=Shutouts, ERA=Earned Run Average. **League's worst totals are shown in boldface type.**

Outfielder Danny Murphy (second from left) squeezes into a photo session of the A's $100,000 infield. Left to right: first baseman Stuffy McInnis, Murphy, third baseman Home Run Baker, shortstop John Barry, and second baseman Eddie Collins.

★★★ **6** ★★★

From Champs to Chumps

The 1916 Philadelphia A's

In 1914 Connie Mack seemed to have the game of baseball all figured out. He had stuffed his Philadelphia A's so full of talent that there seemed to be no end in sight to their championships. League rivals, struggling to catch the magnificent A's, only siipped further behind each year. Philadelphia could call on not one but two of the best pitchers the game had ever seen: Chief Bender and Eddie Plank. Backing them up were Eddie Collins and Home-Run Baker of the $100,000 infield (a lot of money at that time) and a solid outfield.

But the smug A's found a surprise waiting for them in the World Series. Boston's unlikely Braves rose up to beat the defending Series champs in four straight games. Like a punctured balloon, the high-flying A's crashed down to earth. In one year, they fell from a 99-53 record to 43-109. The next

season, they hit bottom, winning recognition as the worst outfit to set foot on an American League field. The A's were so terrible that in nearly 70 years no team has seriously challenged them for that unwanted title.

It's often hard to pinpoint just what makes a team fall apart, but, in this case, it was clear. Connie Mack, the genius who built the championship team, simply tore it apart. Although no one knows all the reasons for his actions, two things stand out. First, Mack was upset with his players for their 1914 disaster. In his opinion, they hadn't put out a full effort. Secondly, Mack always had an eye on the cashbox. When the new Federal League started a bidding war over major league players, the tight-fisted Mack refused to be drawn in. In fact, it looked like a perfect time to sell his players.

After the Federal League signed star pitchers Bender and Plank in 1915, Mack peddled most of his other men to wealthier owners. His hottest product, Eddie Collins, brought in $50,000 from the Chicago White Sox. Altogether, Connie Mack made around $180,000 on the sale of his players, and he also cut his payroll to almost nothing.

Connie's bank book may have never looked better, but his ball club had never looked worse. Only three quality players from 1914 were still on the team in 1916. First baseman Stuffy McInnis, a .300 hitter still in the prime of his career, was the only one who remained from the $100,000 infield. Underrated outfielder Amos Strunk still prowled the A's outfield, and the pitching staff was gone except for Bullet Joe Bush. Bush, a man with a tricky combination of a hard fastball and a forkball, won 196 games in his career. Later he would go on to post a 26-7 mark in a season with the New York Yankees. But as he was to find out, this 1916 A's team was a far cry from the Yankees.

Philadelphia's wholesale shuffling of players left them without a third baseman or shortstop of any description.

By 1916 the $100,000 infield had plunged to bargain basement values. Of the original four, only McInnis (above) remained.

Connie Mack tried to get through the season with outfielder Lawton "Whitey" Witt at the important shortstop position and another outfielder, Charlie Pick, was handed the third-base job. The confidence of the A's pitchers could not have been helped by the sight of these reluctant outfielders manning the left side of the infield!

With Nap Lajoie on the roster, second base may have seemed like it was in good hands. Lajoie, after all, had once hit .422. But Lajoie had reached that mark 15 years earlier. In 1916 at age 40, he couldn't cover much ground and could no longer get the bat around a fastball. The same could be said of Rube Oldring, an outfielder who showed the effects of his 11 seasons in the league.

Rounding out the club were right fielder Jimmy Walsh, who had hit only .206 the year before, and "utter confusion" at catcher. Second-year man Billy Meyer held the starting job on the "strength" of his .232 batting average. But once he was lost to an appendix operation in July, it was anyone's guess who would catch. Pitchers complained of going to the mound and finding total strangers behind the plate. Typical of

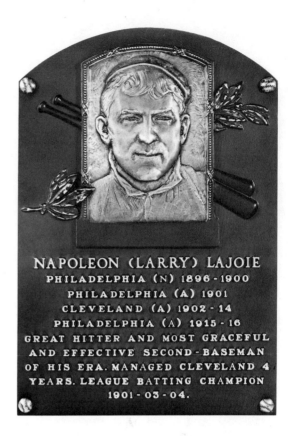

NAPOLEON (LARRY) LAJOIE
PHILADELPHIA (N) 1896-1900
PHILADELPHIA (A) 1901
CLEVELAND (A) 1902-14
PHILADELPHIA (A) 1915-16
GREAT HITTER AND MOST GRACEFUL
AND EFFECTIVE SECOND-BASEMAN
OF HIS ERA. MANAGED CLEVELAND 4
YEARS. LEAGUE BATTING CHAMPION
1901-03-04.

the recruits scoured up by the A's was Ralph (Doc) Carroll. After putting in 10 games with the club, Doc called it a career with a .091 average.

Pitchers like Bullet Joe Bush looked around at their fielders as if they were seeing their new house destroyed by fire. Still, both Bush and rookie Elmer Myers fought gamely against the odds. Between them, they won 29 of the team's 36 wins, with Bush going 15-22 with a 2.57 ERA, and Myers at 14-23 and 3.66. When those two weren't on the mound, though, the A's could just as well have stayed at home. The combined record of the rest of the staff was 7-72!

Two of the Philadelphia starters found themselves in a jinxed race as exciting as the later home-run contests of Maris/Mantle and Ruth/Gehrig. Jack Nabors and Tom Sheehan, both second-year men, shared a room on the road. If it's true that misery loves company, it was a good match. Sheehan and Nabors fell into a neck-and-neck race for the worst pitching record of all time. Sheehan allowed a respectable 3.69 earned runs per game, yet finished with a 1-16 record. But even he was living a charmed life compared to the snakebitten Nabors. With a 3.47 ERA, he hardly deserved to be saddled with a 1-19 mark.

Nabors' 19-game losing streak apparently took its toll. After working eight masterful innings one steamy day, Jack carried a 1-0 lead into the ninth. He well deserved his second win of the season but was done in by sloppy fielding. Two errors gave away the tying run and put a runner on third base. The pitcher promptly launched the wildest pitch in history, far over the catcher's head, and allowed the winning run to

Tom Sheehan did not win a game in 15 decisions as a starting pitcher in 1916. His only victory came in relief.

score. Nabors reportedly explained that he wasn't about to slave away in that heat for a team that wasn't going to score anyway! In Nabors' case, such bitterness was at least understandable, as he finished his career at 1-24.

The two capable players still in their prime, McInnis and Strunk, chipped in their fair share with .295 and .316 averages. But no other starters topped .247, and the A's tied for last in the league in batting. While the pitchers also ranked at the bottom in ERA, the A's trademark was the booted ball. Botching 1 out of every 20 chances, they had to have been the worst fielding club in modern times. With their shifted outfielders making 120 infield errors, the A's collected 314 errors, 66 more than any other American League team.

Other notable "achievements" included 20 losses in a row and a 36-117 mark, both of which are the worst ever in the American League. Perhaps the best example of how bad the A's were is the fact that they finished 40 games behind the next worst team! In his fall from first to last place, Connie Mack demonstrated clearly who really controls the fortunes of a major league club.

That season Amos Strunk took fourth place in the American League batting race with his .316 average.

Two years after proudly hosting the best team in baseball, Philadelphia's Scribe Park turned into a house of horrors.

THE 1916 PHILADELPHIA A'S

Losing Season Streak: 1915-1924 10 years
Last Place Streak: 1915-1921 7 years

1916 Record: 36-117 (54.5 games behind Boston Red Sox)

	R*	OR	BA	HR	SB	E	CG	ShO	ERA
Boston	548	480	.248	14	**129**	183	76	23	2.48
Chicago	601	500	.251	17	197	203	73	18	2.36
Detroit	673	573	.264	17	190	211	81	9	2.97
New York	575	561	.246	34	179	219	83	10	2.77
St. Louis	591	545	.245	13	234	248	71	9	2.58
Cleveland	630	621	.250	16	160	232	**65**	9	.2.99
Washington	534	543	**.242**	**12**	185	231	84	11	2.66
Philadelphia	**447**	**776**	**.242**	19	151	**314**	94	11	**3.84**

Starting Lineup:

	Position	Bat Average	HR	Errors
Stuffy McInnis	1B	.295	1	12
Nap Lajoie	2B	.246	2	16
Whitey Witt	SS	.245	2	78**
Charlie Pick	3B	.241	1	42**
Jimmy Walsh	RF	.233	1	12
Amos Strunk	CF	.316	3	7
Rube Oldring	LF	.247	0	8
Billy Meyer	C	.232	1	12

**most in league at that position

Starting Pitchers:

	Wins	Loses	ERA
Bullet Joe Bush	15	22	2.57
Elmer Myers	14	23	3.66
Jack Nabors	1	19	3.47
Tom Sheehan	1	16	3.69
Jing Johnson	2	10	3.74

Relief Pitchers: NONE

* R=Runs Scored, OR=Opponents' Runs Scored, BA=Batting Average, HR=Home Runs, SB=Stolen Bases, E=Errors, CG=Complete Games, ShO=Shutouts, ERA=Earned Run Average. **League's worst totals are shown in boldface type.**

In 1962 "Marvelous" Marv Throneberry returned to New York, where he had produced
a .037 average as a pinch hitter for the Yankees in the late 1950s.
Life didn't get any better for him the second time around.

★★★ **7** ★★★

"Can't Anybody Here Play This Game?"

The 1962 New York Mets

One of the first rules of pro sports is that fans love a winner. If you have no star players and little hope of winning, fans won't waste their time coming to games. In baseball, however, there has been one glaring exception to this rule. The 1962 New York Mets were so terrible that fans actually rushed to the park to see for themselves if they were really as bad as everyone said. And the Mets rarely disappointed them! The brand-new New York outfit turned losing into an art by coming up with countless ways to blow a ball game. In the club's first four seasons, they lost 452 games, an average of 113 per year! Only their sense of humor and the fans' curiosity saved them from total disaster.

The entire National League must share the blame for the pitiful start of the Mets. When the league expanded from 8 to 10 teams in 1962, they weren't sure how to go about it. After all, they hadn't added any new clubs since the last century. One thing they all agreed on was that they weren't going to hand the new Mets or the Houston Colt 45's a winning lineup. They wanted to give them just enough talent to help make them competitive. In the case of the Mets, they far undershot that goal.

For the price of about $1.8 million, the Mets were allowed to choose from a list of well-worn veterans, reserves clinging to their rosters by a thread, untested or unpromising rookies, or the injured. In other words, they paid a fortune for players no one particularly wanted. It was like trying to build a high-rise building out of sand.

Sifting through the lists of "who isn't who," New York found a few veteran hitters with a couple of swings left in their careers. The Chicago Cubs had no further use for Richie Ashburn, a 15-year veteran in the outfield. Although a lifetime .308 hitter, Richie had slowed to .257 in 1961. He would be lucky to last the season. Gil Hodges was a popular choice for fans who remembered his All-Star play at first base for the Brooklyn Dodgers. But Gil was 38 years old on opening day of 1962, and he had managed only .198 and .242 in the last two seasons.

Other men with big-league experience who came to the Mets were shortstop Elio Chacon from Cincinnati, second baseman Charlie Neal from Los Angeles, third baseman Felix Mantilla from Milwaukee, and catcher Chris Cannizzaro from St. Louis. All had been reserves, but they would be pushed into the starting lineup in New York.

New York did manage to buy hard-hitting outfielder Frank Thomas from the Braves. Although a shakey fielder, Thomas had hit a .284 with 25 home runs the year before. New York also brought in a pair of infielders named Marv Throneberry and Rod Kanehl. Scouts had suspected that both were capable of hitting in the big leagues,

Was this the same Roger Craig who fired four shutouts and chalked up an 11-5 mark with a 2.06 ERA for the champion Dodgers in 1959?

but they had little to offer in the field. Throneberry had not been able to crack the lineup of the awful Kansas City A's, but he won the first-base job with the Mets.

Weak as the batting order may have looked, it was brimming with talent compared to what the Mets found in the pitching department. The top man was Roger Craig, a seven-year veteran of the Dodgers, whose most recent

60

record was 5-6 with a 6.15 ERA. A promising Pirate lefty named Al Jackson could have used another year in the minors to develop, but the Mets needed him right away as their number-two starter. They also made a full-time starter out of Cincinnati's Jay Hook, who had given up 83 hits in 63 innings the year before on his way to a 7.76 ERA. Finally, the Mets came up with a pair of St. Louis hurlers, Craig Anderson and Robert L. (Bob) Miller, who won a total of five games between them in 1961.

The job of molding this group into a major league team was given to 71-year-old Casey Stengel, already a baseball legend. The Mets hoped he could draw on his years as manager of the mighty Yankees to point the way for his players. As it happened, the Old Professor's years as manager of the losing Boston Braves in the 1940s were better preparation for what he was about to go through!

The high point of the season for the Mets was opening day. They didn't win, but they didn't lose either: the game was rained out! The postponement was like a stay of execution. Thrown into big-league action against the Cardinals,

Even a good pitcher needs an able infield to back him up. That's why Al Jackson lost 73 games in his four years with the Mets.

New York lost, 11-4. From the start, they played a style of ball that reminded writers of men trying to learn a game in a foreign country. Three errors and a balk contributed to their first defeat.

Perhaps it was only a coincidence that the Mets opened their home season on Friday the 13th. Their ballpark was a fitting showcase for a team of their quality. The old Polo Grounds, due to be destroyed in two years, had been dusted off for use while a new stadium was being built. Thanks to three wild pitches, New York treated their fans to a 4-3 loss to the Pirates at the home opener.

Stengel and the Mets knew they were in for a long season when they lost their first 9 games. Fortunately, they could see the humor in their hopeless situation. While playing their best, the Mets contributed their own wisecracks to those of the press. Stengel managed to keep a straight face as he noted that his team had a shot at losing *all* 162 games!

But an unlikely burst of hitting and pitching in the 10th game caused the Mets to smash the Pirates, 9-1, for their first win. They continued to show flashes of good play throughout the summer, but New York fans never knew when a close game would be lost due to another Met mistake. The Mets lost one game when *four* of their runners were thrown out at the plate! Another close game got away when the catcher fired a pick-off throw past the first baseman. Other contests were ruined when inexperienced Mets missed the coaches' signals. Bill Veeck, who once ran the hapless St. Louis Browns, admitted that the Mets were far worse than any of his cellar-dwellers. Manager Stengel summed it up best when, after another frustrating chain of blunders, he muttered, "Can't anybody here play this game?"

The Mets' awkward style of play attracted more fans than any loser in the game's history: nearly a million in that first year. Many of them came to see Marvelous Marv Throneberry, who had become the symbol of the Mets. Marv made 17 errors at first base, including an underhand toss that he flipped over the pitcher's head on an easy play at first base. Another time he determinedly ran down a runner caught in a rundown between first and second base while the runner on third base trotted home to score the winning run!

To put it kindly, Rod ("Hot Rod") Kanehl could play all the infield positions as well as he could play the outfield.

Although used mostly as a backup, Kanehl managed to collect 32 errors.

Fans interested in statistics had fun keeping track of the Mets' various losing streaks. The team's worst stretch brought 17 losses in a row. The two ex-Cardinals, Miller and Anderson, suffered through terrible slumps. Miller lost 12 in a row during the year, and Anderson topped

Starting did not agree with Craig Anderson. After a fine season working out of the St. Louis bullpen, he was winless in 17 starts as a Met.

Met fans' favorite story, though, was the day Marv hit a clutch triple against the Cubs. Unfortunately, he missed first base by a couple of feet. He was called out, and his mistake cost the Mets the game.

When his teammates pulled similar goofs, Throneberry complained that they were stealing his fans. Hot Rod Kanehl was his closest competitor.

that with 16 straight losses. Anderson finished at 3-17 and pitched only briefly for two more years without winning another game. Miller's 1-12 mark propelled him on a record-setting trip around the majors. The right-hander changed teams 12 times in his career.

Other Met hurlers were in no position to criticize those two. Roger Craig led the team in wins with 10, but he had to suffer through 24 losses to reach that mark. He also treated National League batters to 35 home runs. Al Jackson sported an 8-20 mark, and Jay Hook just missed giving the club three 20-game losers with his 8-19 record.

By finishing at 40-120, 60½ games behind the Giants, New York claimed the modern major league record for losses in a season. Their .240 average (21 points below the league average), 5.04 ERA (1.10 above the average), and .967 fielding average put them last in all three major categories.

Those who wondered if the amazing Mets had any last tricks left for their final game were not disappointed. The Mets staged a rally late in the game, only to lose when they hit into a triple play. The Mets had done it again!

The Mets were the worst major league baseball team in this century, "And you could look it up," to use Casey Stengel's favorite phrase.

THE 1962 NEW YORK METS

Losing Record Streak: 1962-1968   7 years
Last Place Streak: 1962-1965   4 years

1962 Record: 40-120 (60.5 games behind San Francisco Giants)

	R*	OR	BA	HR	SB	E	CG	ShO	ERA
San Francisco	878	690	.278	204	73	142	62	10	3.79
Los Angeles	842	697	.268	140	198	193	44	8	3.62
Cincinnati	802	685	270	167	66	145	51	13	3.75
Pittsburgh	706	626	.268	108	50	152	40	13	3.37
Milwaukee	730	665	.252	181	57	124	59	10	3.68
St. Louis	774	664	.271	137	86	132	53	17	3.55
Philadelphia	705	759	.260	142	79	138	43	7	4.28
Houston	**592**	717	.246	**105**	**42**	173	34	9	3.83
Chicago	632	827	.253	126	78	146	**29**	**4**	4.54
New York	617	**948**	**.240**	139	59	**210**	43	**4**	**5.04**

		Position	Bat Average	HR	Errors
Starting Lineup:	Marv Throneberry	1B	.244	16	17**
	Charlie Neal	2B	.260	11	13
	Elio Chacon	SS	.236	2	22
	Felix Mantilla	3B	.275	11	14
	Richie Ashburn	RF	.306	7	5
	Jim Hickman	CF	.245	13	8
	Frank Thomas	LF	.266	34	9
	Chris Cannizzaro	C	.241	0	7

**most in league at that position

		Wins	Loses	ERA	Saves
Starting Pitchers:	Roger Craig	10	24	4.51	
	Al Jackson	8	20	4.40	
	Jay Hook	8	19	4.84	
	Bob Miller	1	12	4.89	
Relief Pitchers:	Craig Anderson	3	17	5.35	4
	Ken MacKenzie	5	4	4.95	1
	Bob Moorhead	0	2	4.53	0

* R=Runs Scored, OR=Opponents' Runs Scored, BA=Batting Average, HR=Home Runs, SB=Stolen Bases, E=Errors, CG=Complete Games, ShO=Shutouts, ERA=Earned Run Average. **League's worst totals are shown in boldface type.**

DENTON T. (CY) YOUNG
CLEVELAND (N) 1890-98
ST. LOUIS (N) 1899-1900
BOSTON (A) 1901-08
CLEVELAND (A) 1909-11
BOSTON (N) 1911
ONLY PITCHER IN FIRST HUNDRED
YEARS OF BASEBALL TO WIN 500 GAMES.
AMONG HIS 511 VICTORIES WERE 3
NO-HIT SHUTOUTS. PITCHED PERFECT
GAME MAY 5, 1904, NO OPPOSING
BATSMAN REACHING FIRST BASE.

JESSE C. BURKETT
BATTING STAR WHO PLAYED OUTFIELD FOR
THE NEW YORK, CLEVELAND AND ST. LOUIS
N.L. TEAMS AND THE ST. LOUIS AND BOSTON
A.L. TEAMS. SHARES WITH ROGERS HORNSBY
AND TY COBB THE RECORD OF HITTING .400
OR BETTER THE MOST TIMES. ACCOMPLISHED
THIS ON THREE OCCASIONS. TOPPED THE
N.L. IN HITTING THREE TIMES, BATTING
OVER .400 TO GAIN THE CHAMPIONSHIP
IN 1895 AND 1896.

How did these Hall of Famers get mixed up in the story of baseball's sorriest squad?

Legend has it that the game of baseball was born on this field in Cooperstown, New York, in 1889.
It nearly died of shame in Cleveland in 1899.

★★★ 8 ★★★

In a Class by Themselves

The 1899 Cleveland Spiders

Although the modern age of baseball began in 1901, there was a team in 1899 that was so horrible it simply cannot be left out of this book. The Cleveland Spiders were the most embarrassing blot on the pages of baseball history, and their story is all the more bizarre because they performed *exactly* as their owner hoped they would. Caught in a war of spite between fans and the club owner, the Spiders of 1899 set records for poor play that will never be equalled.

It all started when Frank Robison, a wealthy Cleveland streetcar-system owner, dreamed of running a baseball club that would become the power of the West. Robison did not quite reach that goal, but his National League team, the Spiders, often made a good run for the pennant. The Spiders were paced by Cy Young, who won more games in his career than any other pitcher. Young

had earned a 25-14 mark in 1898, his eighth-straight season over the 20-win level. Following closely was Jack Powell, who had won 24 and lost 15 for the Spiders that year. For fans who liked explosive batting mixed with their pitchers' duels, the Spiders offered Jesse Burkett. A lifetime average of .340 would later put Burkett in baseball's Hall of Fame.

Young, Powell, Burkett, and their teammates powered the Spiders to an 81-68 record in 1898, good for fifth place in the 12-team league. Cleveland fans, however, had not been rushing to the stadium. With attendance lagging at only 70,000 late in the season, owner Robison chose to play the remaining games on the road.

Fuming over the poor attendance, Robison found a way to get revenge. While still owning the Spiders, he bought

Jesse "The Crab" Burkett (left) hit .402 during his old team's embarrassing year. John Powell (above) got caught in his owner's last efforts to draw fans before giving up on Cleveland. Playing pro ball on Sunday was not allowed in the 19th century and when the Spiders tried to boost attendance by doing so, pitcher Powell was arrested, tried, convicted of the crime, and fined.

the bumbling St. Louis Browns at a cheap price. At a time when league meetings were sometimes settled by fistfights, Robison got the rest of the owners to approve that shady operation. Robison then moved Young, Powell, Burkett, and any other promising Spider to St. Louis.

Cleveland's top four pitchers and seven of their eight starters in the field took the train to St. Louis.

To get an idea of the talent left in Cleveland, consider the case of catcher Lou Criger. With more than 2,500 at bats, Criger owns the ninth worst batting average in baseball history: .221. Yet he was one of those who was promoted! Cleveland then became like Siberia for nervous St. Louis players, who were warned they would be sent to Cleveland if they didn't play well.

Robison left the Cleveland mess in the hands of his brother and sat back to enjoy his revenge. It turned out to be a costly bit of spite. Cleveland fans, aware of what was happening, refused to go to the games. Attendance for the first 24 home games averaged less than 200. When visiting teams complained about losing money on trips to Cleveland's empty park, the club had to cancel the rest of its home games. The Spiders became known as the "Misfits" and spent the rest of the year on the road.

Only once during the 154-game schedule did Cleveland win 2 games in a row. Rival clubs thought so little of the Spiders that one pitcher was suspended for a month just for losing a game to them!

Caught in the middle of this disaster were the players. Three of them were veterans who deserved better treatment at the end of their careers. Joe Quinn, an able second baseman winding down his 17-year career; first baseman Tommy Tucker, in his last of 13 seasons; and center fielder Tommy Dowd, who had once hit .323, must have wondered what had happened to the game they loved. Quinn, with his .286 average, was the closest thing Cleveland had to a bright spot. For his courageous showing, he was "rewarded" by being named manager two months into the season. It was his privilege to direct a team that totally fell apart. After an 8-30 start, Cleveland slipped to 18-82 and then won only 2 of their last 54 games!

The list of unknown players and their performances is almost too ridiculous to believe. The ace of the pitching staff was Jim "Cold Water" Hughey. His 7-24 record for St. Louis in 1898 had doomed him to spend 1899 with Cleveland. There the five-year veteran became a baseball rarity: a 30-game loser. He watched base hits crack off opponents' bats with machine-gun regularity: 403 hits in 283 innings. Hughey won 4 and lost 30 with a 5.41 ERA.

Frank Bates was pounded for hits nearly every time he threw a strike, which wasn't that often. On his way to a 1-18 record and a 7.24 ERA with Cleveland, Bates walked 110 batters in 162 innings, and struck out only 13. A Purple Heart medal should have gone to Charlie Knepper for courage in the face of hardship. Despite being roughed up for a 4-22 record and a 5.78 ERA, Charlie completed all 26 of his starts. Then there was Crazy Schmidt, whose 2-17 and 5.86 figures could have driven anyone out of his mind.

The strangest pitcher of all, however, was Harry Colliflower. An amateur pitcher, Colliflower happened to be passing through town when the desperate Spiders talked him into pitching a game for them. After winning his first game, Colliflower was signed to a contract. He should have quit while he was ahead, though. Harry never again won a major league game, and he finished the year with a 1-11 mark and an eye-popping 8.17 ERA.

The hitters weren't as spectacular in their failures. Instead they were consistently poor, with averages ranging from .237 to .286. No one on the roster hit more than two home runs. The fielding was no better, as shortstop Harry Lockhead kept busy flubbing 81 chances. Left fielder Dick Harley somehow turned a relatively safe position into a circus with 27 errors.

When the season finally ended, it was not a moment too soon. Spider games had become almost too brutal for a sporting person to sit through. Cleveland ended its season in style, losing to sixth-place Cincinnati by scores of 16-3 and 19-1.

While the former Spider stars boosted St. Louis to an 84-67 mark, Cleveland wound up at 20-134, 84 games behind first-place Brooklyn. Cleveland's team batting average of .253 may not seem bad, but it was 29 points below the league average. There was nothing respectable about the pitching statistics, either. Cleveland's 6.37 ERA was 2½ runs per game above the league average.

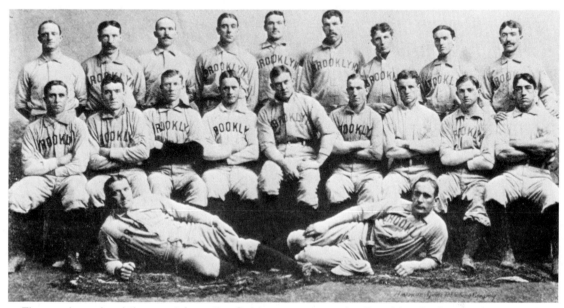
Those who gained the most from the Spider mess were the Brooklyn Dodgers, who won 101 games in 1899 and lost only 47.

Thankfully, the Spiders broke up at the end of the season, and baseball's disgrace, brought about by irresponsible ownership, was wiped from the slate. Within two years, Cleveland had a new team, which came to be known as the Indians. Quickly and quietly, the dreadful story of the Cleveland Spiders was shoved aside, and the worst team in baseball was forgotten by all but a few history-minded fans.

THE 1899 CLEVELAND SPIDERS

Losing Record Streak: 1899   1 year
Last Place Streak: 1899   1 year

1899 Record: 20-134 (84 games behind Brooklyn Dodgers)

	R*	OR	BA	HR	SB	E	CG	ShO	ERA
Brooklyn	892	658	.291	26	271	314	121	9	3.25
Boston	858	645	.287	40	185	303	138	13	3.26
Philadelphia	916	743	.301	30	212	379	129	15	3.47
Baltimore	827	691	.297	17	364	308	133	9	3.31
St. Louis	819	739	.285	46	210	397	134	7	3.36
Cincinnati	856	770	.275	13	228	339	130	8	3.70
Pittsburgh	834	765	.289	27	179	361	**117**	9	3.60
Chicago	812	763	.277	27	247	428	147	8	3.37
Louisville	827	775	.280	40	233	394	134	5	3.45
New York	734	863	.281	23	234	**433**	138	4	4.29
Washington	743	983	.272	47	176	403	131	3	4.93
Cleveland	**529**	1252	**.253**	**12**	**127**	388	138	**0**	**6.37**

		Position	Bat Average	HR	Errors
Starting Lineup:	Tommy Tucker	1B	.241	0	30
	Joe Quinn	2B	.286	0	31
	Harry Lockhead	SS	.238	1	81
	Sutter Sullivan	3B	.245	0	23
	Sport McAllister	RF	.237	1	7
	Tommy Dowd	CF	.278	2	17
	Dick Harley	LF	.250	1	27**
	Joe Sugden	C	.276	0	21

**most in league at that position

		Wins	Loses	ERA
Starting Pitchers:	Cold Water Hughey	4	30	5.41
	Charlie Knepper	4	22	5.78
	Frank Bates	1	18	7.24
	Crazy Schmidt	2	17	5.86
	Harry Colliflower	1	11	8.17
	Wee Willie Sudhoff	3	8	6.98

Relief Pitchers: NONE

* R=Runs Scored, OR=Opponents' Runs Scored, BA=Batting Average, HR=Home Runs, SB=Stolen Bases, E=Errors,
CG=Complete Games, ShO=Shutouts, ERA=Earned Run Average. **League's worst totals are shown in boldface type.**